A Note from
Mary Pope Osborne About the

MAGIC TREE HOUSE® FACT TRACKERS

When I write Magic Tree House® adventures, I love including facts about the times and places Jack and Annie visit. But when readers finish these adventures, I want them to learn even more. So that's why we write a series of nonfiction books that are companions to the fiction titles in the Magic Tree House® series. We call these books Fact Trackers because we love to track the facts! Whether we're researching dinosaurs, pyramids, Pilgrims, sea monsters, or cobras, we're always amazed at how wondrous and surprising the real world is. We want you to experience the same wonder we do—so get out your pencils and notebooks and hit the trail with us. You can be a Magic Tree House® Fact Tracker, too!

Mary Pope Osborne

Here's what kids, parents, and teachers have to say about the Magic Tree House® Fact Trackers:

"They are so good. I can't wait for the next one. All I can say for now is prepare to be amazed!" —Alexander N.

"I have read every Magic Tree House book there is. The [Fact Trackers] are a thrilling way to get more information about the special events in the story." —John R.

"These are fascinating nonfiction books that enhance the magical time-traveling adventures of Jack and Annie. I love these books, especially *American Revolution*. I was learning so much, and I didn't even know it!" —Tori Beth S.

"[They] are an excellent 'behind-the-scenes' look at what the [Magic Tree House fiction] has started in your imagination! You can't buy one without the other; they are such a complement to one another." —Erika N., mom

"Magic Tree House [Fact Trackers] took my children on a journey from Frog Creek, Pennsylvania, to so many significant historical events! The detailed manuals are a remarkable addition to the classic fiction Magic Tree House books we adore!" —Jenny S., mom

"[They] are very useful tools in my classroom, as they allow for students to be part of the planning process. Together, we find facts in the [Fact Trackers] to extend the learning introduced in the fictional companions. Researching and planning classroom activities, such as our class Olympics based on facts found in *Ancient Greece and the Olympics*, help create a genuine love for learning!" —Paula H., teacher

MAGIC TREE HOUSE®
FACT TRACKER

Snow Leopards and Other Wild Cats

A NONFICTION COMPANION TO MAGIC TREE HOUSE #36:

Sunlight on the Snow Leopard

BY MARY POPE OSBORNE
AND JENNY LAIRD

ILLUSTRATED BY ISIDRE MONÉS

A STEPPING STONE BOOK™

Random House 🏠 New York

Visit us on the Web!
MagicTreeHouse.com
rhcbooks.com

Educators and librarians, for a variety of teaching tools, visit us at
RHTeachersLibrarians.com

Library of Congress Cataloging-in-Publication Data
Names: Osborne, Mary Pope, author. | Laird, Jenny, author. | Mones, Isidre, illustrator.
Title: Snow leopards and other wild cats / by Mary Pope Osborne and Jenny Laird ;
illustrated by Isidre Mones.
Description: New York : Random House Children's Books, [2022] | Series: Magic tree
house fact tracker ; 44 | A nonfiction companion to Magic Tree House #36: Sunlight on
the snow leopard. | Includes bibliographical references and index. | Audience: Ages 7–10
Summary: "A nonfiction book about snow leopards and other wild cats"
—Provided by publisher.
Identifiers: LCCN 2021044059 | ISBN 978-1-9848-9326-0 (trade) |
ISBN 978-1-9848-9327-7 (lib. bdg.) | ISBN 978-1-9848-9328-4 (ebook)
Subjects: LCSH: Snow leopard—Juvenile literature. | Wildcat—Juvenile literature.
Classification: LCC QL737.C23 O825 2022 | DDC 599.75/55—dc23

Printed in the United States of America

10 9 8 7 6 5 4 3 2 1

This book has been officially leveled by using the F&P Text Level Gradient™ Leveling
System.

For Hayden Courts, the coolest cat I know

Scientific Consultant:

MARCELLA J. KELLY, PhD, Department of Fish and Wildlife Conservation, Virginia Tech

Education Consultant:

HEIDI JOHNSON, language acquisition and science education specialist

Special thanks to the Random House team: Mallory Loehr, Jenna Lettice, Isidre Monés, Polo Orozco, Jason Zamajtuk, and especially to our beloved editor, Diane Landolf

Snow Leopards and Other Wild Cats

Contents

Dear Readers,

In <u>Sunlight on the Snow Leopard</u>, we met a mysterious snow leopard in the Himalayas. Snow leopards are beautiful, shy creatures that are rarely seen. When we came home, we couldn't wait to track more facts about snow leopards and other wild cats, as well.

We checked out some great books from the library. Then we did more research on the computer. We learned that there are lots of different kinds of wild cats in the world. Some of them are as big as bears, and some of them are as small as guinea pigs! Having cats around helps keep the whole world

healthy. But many cats are in danger of disappearing forever. Including snow leopards.

Some people are working hard to help wild cats survive. Just read about the monks in the Himalayas who have become the protectors of snow leopards.

So pull out your notebooks and become fact trackers like us. With all the things you learn about these amazing creatures, you'll know why we're so wild about cats! And you'll know why it is important to work together to protect them.

Jack   Annie

1

Cats of the World

Cats have been roaming the earth much longer than humans. The very first members of the cat family, or *felines*, appeared about 25 million years ago. Early cat fossils have been found in almost all parts of the world.

Some of the most common prehistoric felines were saber-toothed cats. These fierce animals had up to eight-inch-long fangs that were jagged like a steak knife. They could use their long, sharp teeth to quickly kill large animals with just one bite to the throat.

Some kinds of saber-toothed cats had bodies that were built more like bears. They had short legs, huge paws, and razor-sharp claws.

This saber-toothed cat fossil was found in a tar pit in California.

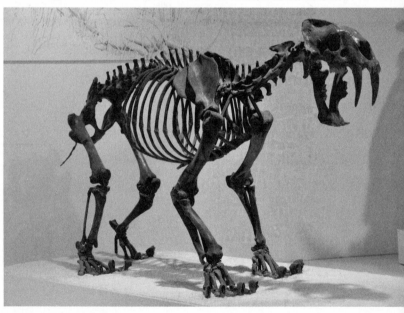

Over millions of years, cats developed amazing hunting *instincts*. They have some of the most graceful, athletic bodies in nature.

About 12,000 years ago, some of these wild creatures started to form a relationship with people. As humans began growing crops for food, they needed to store their grains. But rats and mice were drawn to those grain stores. Cats to the rescue!

Instincts are natural ways of acting that animals are born with.

Domesticated Cats

Cats are great hunters, but they also love an easy meal. As rodents flocked to the farms, cats did, too. Cats moved close to people for the huge numbers of rodents to prey on. In return, early farmers let the cats hang around for the free pest control.

Domesticated animals are those that have been tamed and kept by humans as pets, work animals, or sources of food.

By the time of the ancient Egyptians, about 4,500 years ago, some cats had been *domesticated,* or brought inside the home. The cats of ancient Egypt were pampered pets. They sometimes wore jewels. Wealthy people mummified their cats and buried them in special tombs.

16

Today's Pets

These days, cats are the most popular pets in the world! Dogs may be man's best friend, but across the globe, people have more cats in their homes than any other animal.

Although the cats that share our homes are domesticated, at times, they do some wild things. Have you ever wondered why cats scratch at furniture? Or attack a ball of yarn?

These actions are a lot like the survival behaviors of wild cats. Our pet cats come from fierce ancestors. So, even though they no longer need to hunt for their meals, they haven't lost their wild cat instincts.

Cats have scent glands in their paws. Wild cats scratch trees to mark their territory with their smell and with claw marks.

The bark also keeps their claws clean and sharp.

Things that move or dangle look like food or danger to cats. In the wild, cats compete with snakes for food, so anything shaped like a snake wakes up their fighting instincts!

A <u>species</u> is a group of plants or animals that are alike in certain ways.

Wild Cats

Today there are about thirty-six different *species,* or kinds, of wild cats in the world.

18

They live on every continent except Australia and Antarctica.

Most cat species thrive where there are plenty of trees. But some do well in open prairies, *savannas,* or even deserts. Many live where it's warm, but others survive well in cold weather.

Some species can live in many kinds of *habitats.* You might picture tigers in a rain forest, but they also live in mountains that are rocky.

A <u>savanna</u> is a grassy plain with few trees.

A <u>habitat</u> is a place where certain animals live, which has the climate, food, water, and plants they need to survive.

19

Big and Small Cats

Wild cats come in all different sizes: small, medium, and huge! But they are often divided into just two groups: big cats and small cats. Or sometimes, roaring cats and purring cats.

Why? Because there are only four kinds of cats that can roar, and they are also the largest felines in the cat family. So most scientists use the term *big cats* to refer to the cats that can roar—tigers, lions, jaguars, and leopards—and *small cats* to refer to the cats that can purr but cannot roar.

Only cats and their near relatives can purr. Big cats can roar because they have a special U-shaped bone in their throats.

Snow leopards are an unusual case. They make a purrlike noise, but it doesn't sound like the purring of small cats. And they can't roar. But, because they are very closely related to the cats that do roar, most scientists agree snow leopards belong in the big cat group.

<u>Big Cats</u>
Lions
Tigers
Jaguars
Leopards
Snow leopards

Sorting cats into groups can get tricky, but all cats, large and small, belong to one big family. Scientists call it the Felidae family.

The black-footed cat of Africa weighs about four pounds. The Siberian tiger weighs up to 700 pounds. Believe it or not, these cats are related!

Hungry Hunters

Big and small cats have a lot of things in common. All cats are expert hunters. This is important because all cats are also *true carnivores* (KAR-nuh-vorz). Animals that mostly eat meat are called carnivores. A true carnivore is an animal that *must* eat meat to get all the nutrition it needs to survive. Some carnivores, like dogs, could survive without meat if they had to. But cats would die without meat.

Cats have rough, raspy tongues for licking meat off bones.

All cats are *predators*. Animals that hunt other animals for food are called predators. The animals they hunt are called *prey*. Some small cats are also prey for larger animals like jackals or foxes. But big cats have no natural predators in the wild.

Only cubs or big cats that are sick or injured are hunted by other predators.

When a species is not preyed upon by other animals, it is an *apex predator. Apex* means the top of something. All big cats are top predators. Apex predators are important for keeping the *ecosystems* around them in balance. Without big cats, many grass-eating animals would overpopulate. This would lead to a lot of damage to the earth. Nature depends on the right balance between predators and prey.

An <u>ecosystem</u> is a network of living things interacting with the nonliving things around them, such as soil, water, and air.

Paws and Claws

Cats have four claws on their back feet and five on their front feet. The extra claw in the front is called a *dew claw.* It is kind of like a human thumb and helps cats get a good grip when catching prey.

Most of the time, cats keep their front

claws pulled back. But when cats need to defend themselves, catch a meal, or climb a tree, their front claws push forward!

Cats have soft pads on their feet so they can quietly sneak up on their prey.

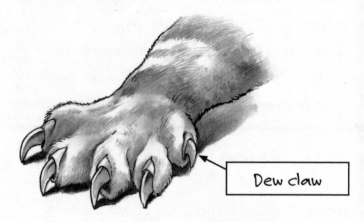

Dew claw

Eyes, Ears, Nose, and Whiskers
Cats use all their senses for hunting. Most hunt at night. They have great night vision. Their eyes can see movement even in near-total darkness.

Cats can sense high-pitched sounds that no human can hear. When a noise interests them, their ears quickly swivel toward the sound.

A house cat's sense of smell is up to 15 times stronger than a human's.

Cats also have a much better sense of smell than humans. Their nose might be their most important organ. They use it to sniff out prey, mates, enemies, friends, and even home territories.

Cats have whiskers on or around their mouths, noses, eyes, chins, and even legs.

Whiskers tell cats if they can fit through a tight space.

Their whiskers tell them a lot. The base of a whisker is full of nerve endings. Whiskers help cats feel their way around, especially in the dark.

Fur

Cat fur comes in all different shades of gray, black, brown, tan, orange, and white. Some coats have stripes or spots. Some have both. Fur can be short and sleek or long and fluffy. Cats that live in cold places have longer, thicker fur to keep warm.

Fur can also be great *camouflage* (KAA-muh-flahj). This means that their natural colors look the same as the world around them. Most cats have fur that blends into the background and lets them hide in plain sight. This is another reason why cats are so good at sneaking up on their prey.

Jaguars are hard to see in the jungle because they have dark spots that fade into the shadows and light-colored fur that blends into the sunlight.

A Clowder of Cats

In the English language, we use special words when we refer to a group or collection of things, people, or animals. These words are called *collective nouns*.

You probably already know a lot of these collective nouns, like:

A *bundle* of firewood
A *bouquet* of flowers
A *pack* of wolves
A *flock* of seagulls

You also probably know that a group of kittens is called a litter. But did you know a group of cats is called a *clowder*? Groups of animals have some of the most fun and interesting names, including these big cats:

A *pride* of lions
A *streak* of tigers
A *leap* of leopards
A *shadow* of jaguars

Snow leopards are the only big cats that don't have a collective noun to talk about them in groups!

2

Snow Leopards

Have you ever seen a snow leopard? If you have, it was probably in a zoo. Very few people ever get to see a snow leopard in the wild. Why? Mainly because these cats live in places far away from where most people live. Snow leopards are found in some of the highest mountain ranges in the world, including the Himalayas and the southern Siberian mountains in Russia.

Snow leopards live in conditions that are among the most extreme on earth!

Another reason snow leopards are rarely seen is that there aren't many to see. Today there are probably fewer than 7,000 snow leopards living in the wild. More than half can be found in China. The rest are spread out over eleven other countries in the central part of Asia.

Cloud Climbers

Snow leopards live higher up than any other cat. In the Himalayas, snow leopards have been found living 18,000 feet above sea level. That's almost four miles high! Most humans will only reach those kinds of heights in an airplane.

Living high up isn't easy for any creature. The climate is cold and dry. The *terrain* is rocky and steep. Food is hard to find. There is less oxygen at higher altitudes, making it harder to breathe. So how do snow leopards manage to survive in areas where no other big cat could? Because of *adaptation* (a-dap-TAY-shun). Over time, their bodies have changed, or *adapted*, to make them perfectly suited for their extreme environment.

Guinness World Records lists the snow leopard as the highest-living land predator.

Terrain is the physical features of a piece of land.

Little Big Cats

Snow leopards are the smallest of the big cats. They are about the height of a golden retriever and weigh between 60 and 120 pounds. Despite their name, snow leopards are more closely related to tigers than leopards. But tigers are the biggest cats in the world. They're a foot taller than snow leopards and weigh *hundreds* of pounds more!

Even though tigers are much larger, their tails are about the same length as snow leopards'!

On average, a snow leopard's body is between three and four feet long. That's only about five to seven pencils laid end to end. This isn't counting the snow leopard's tail, which can be up to three feet long!

Snow leopards aren't as big and powerful as tigers, but they also don't need to eat as much food. Tigers have to eat about fifty large animals a year to survive. Snow leopards can live on as few as twenty. Needing fewer meals is a good survival trait for an animal living in such harsh conditions.

Long Tails

The snow leopard's tail is a wonder. In proportion to its body size, a snow leopard has the longest, thickest tail of any cat!

The tail is thick because it stores fat

for the winter. When food is in short sup-
ply, stored fat can mean the difference between survival and starvation.

For cats, a tail is like a balancing pole
for a tightrope walker. A longer tail means
better balance. All cats are good acrobats,
but snow leopards might be the best. Their
big tails keep them balanced as they leap
across rocky gaps and sprint down dangerously steep rocks.

A snow leopard's tail is almost as long as
its body!

Their long, strong tails help snow leopards make quick, sharp turns.

A snow leopard's tail fur is about 5 inches thick!

The extra-long tails are also extra furry. While sleeping, snow leopards will wrap their bushy tails around their body and face like a scarf. This warms the body and protects the nose from frostbite.

Paws

A snow leopard's paws are two to three times bigger than the average human hand. Wow! That means one paw could cover your whole face! These wide paws are great for gripping rocks and walking on top of snow. A snow leopard can walk in snow up to thirty-three inches deep without sinking! People need snowshoes to walk in snow that deep. Snowshoes are large and flat, which spreads a person's weight over a greater area of snow so their body doesn't sink down. A snow leopard's wide paws do the same thing.

Snow leopard paws are like natural snowshoes!

Fur and More Fur

Snow leopards have the thickest fur of any cat. For every square inch of their body, a snow leopard has 26,000 hairs! A human head only has about 1,300 per square inch! Their fur grows even thicker in the freezing cold winters. But snow leopards have another secret weapon to beat the chill. Hidden underneath their furry coats is a dense, woolly layer called *underfur*. This extra layer helps trap body heat, keeping them even warmer.

Underfur, that's kind of like when I wear thermals under my snow pants!

Snow leopards' fur is not just a warming blanket. It is also an invisibility cloak. Their coats range in color from smoky-gray to creamy-tan. All have dark, round, flower-shaped spots called *rosettes* (roh-ZETZ). Their bellies are white.

Most big cats have gold-colored eyes, but snow leopards have gray and pale-green eyes.

These colors and spots help them blend with the rocks and snow of their environments. Snow leopards' pretty coats make them nearly invisible to their prey—and to humans!

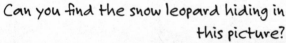

Can you find the snow leopard hiding in this picture?

Say Cheese!

Researchers hide their cameras in stones.

Scientists wanted to know more about these amazing animals. But people can't survive for long in the harsh cold of the snow leopards' home. So how could they get close enough to watch snow leopards in action?

Camera traps!

Camera traps aren't really traps at all. They are digital cameras that can sense when a warm-bodied animal walks by. When snow leopards get near the sensors: *snap!* Capturing images of snow leopards in their natural habitats allows researchers to learn more about these phantom-like felines.

Here's a snow leopard "caught" with a camera trap!

3

Ghosts of the Mountains

The snow leopards' spooky ability to disappear into the rocks and snow has earned them the nickname *ghosts of the mountains*. These "ghosts" seem mysterious because so few people have ever seen one. But snow leopards probably avoid humans mostly because they are shy. If a person approaches them, they simply run away.

Unlike most other big cats, snow leopards don't often fight each other over land or food.

45

Snow leopards also try to avoid one another. Except when females are rearing their young cubs, snow leopards don't have dens or permanent homes. They are almost always on the move. They often have to travel great distances in search of food.

Keep Away

To keep from bumping into another cat along the way, they leave special "keep away" messages. Like many animals, they

This is my tree!

Scratching tree trunk with their claws

will spray rocks and trees with urine to mark their territory.

But snow leopards have other ways to tell other cats that they're in the neighborhood and visitors are not welcome!

This spot is taken!

Rubbing against rocks to leave their scent

Please do not disturb!

...raping the ground
...ith their hind legs

Hunting Habits

Snow leopards sometimes hunt prey three times their own size!

Like all cats, snow leopards are carnivores. They hunt mostly wild sheep and goats for food. But since prey is scarce, they aren't picky and sometimes eat smaller animals like marmots, mice, hares, and even birds.

Snow leopards usually hunt at dusk and dawn. They have great night vision, so they have no trouble walking around in the dark. They sometimes travel many miles in one night.

Bharal, or blue sheep

A snow leopard's nighttime hunt can cover nearly thirty miles. That's a long way to go just to find a meal!

Wow! That's more than a marathon!

Marmot

Asiatic ibex, a wild goat

Once snow leopards are close enough to a prey animal to smell or see it, they usually hide high up in the rocks. They wait for the animal to get within striking distance. And then they pounce! Snow leopards' short, muscular front legs and long, springy back legs are made for leaping and landing with power and grace.

Snow leopards can leap up to ~~fifty feet~~ — or seven times their full length!

In short bursts, snow leopards run about 35–40 miles per hour.

If snow leopards miss their target when they leap, the chase is on! Although goats and sheep are quite nimble on rocky cliffs, they are no match for the cats. Even on steep hills, snow leopards can run forty miles per hour! Once they have captured their prey, snow leopards eat slowly. They hide their catch from other animals and spend the next three or four days finishing their meal.

Cat Courtship

The only time adult snow leopards choose to cross paths is during mating season. Snow leopards breed in the late winter months. Cubs are born in the late spring and early summer. By then it is warm, and there is more food to eat.

When a female snow leopard is ready

to breed, she sprays rocks with her scent to send a message to the males in the area. Once a male and female have found each other, they make soft *chuffing* noises. This is a way to say hi and make friends. Once they have agreed to pair up, they travel together for several days while they mate.

Chuffing is a lot like purring.

After a few days, the male goes back to being on his own. The female finds a place to make a den, usually a cave or rocky shelter. To create a soft nest for her cubs, she lines the floor with fur from her belly. After about three months, she gives birth, usually to two or three cubs.

Cubs

Snow leopard cubs are born small and helpless. At birth, their eyes are closed,

and they only weigh about a pound. That's about the same as a can of soup! After a week or so, snow leopard cubs open their eyes for the first time.

For the next two months, they stay
in the safety of their den. Their mother

returns to the den often to give milk to her cubs. When they are about two months old, the cubs weigh about eight or nine pounds. By then they are strong enough to wander out of their den and begin to eat meat.

When they are between three and four months old, snow leopard cubs stop living in their den. They start following their mother as they hunt for the family's food. Little by little, they learn how to track their prey and how to sneak up on it.

It takes nearly two years for young snow leopards to learn to hunt and survive on their own! After that, the mother cats separate from their young. Each sibling goes off on its own. Young snow leopards usually travel great distances to find their own homes.

Female snow leopards give birth every other year.

The mothers are then ready to mate again and raise a new litter of cubs.

Saving the Species

Snow leopards are built to survive, but as a species, they are at risk of dying out. Sadly, humans pose the biggest threat to snow leopards. *Poachers* hunt these beautiful creatures to sell their fur for lots of money. People destroy snow leopards' habitats by building mines, factories, and farms. Sheep and goat herders sometimes kill snow leopards that attack their livestock.

Poachers are people who hunt or trap animals illegally.

Zoos play a big part in helping to make sure the snow leopard species survives. There are about 700 snow leopards living in zoos around the world.

56

In North America and in Europe, zoos work together to run breeding programs.

Since the 1960s, the Bronx Zoo in New York has helped breed seventy-five healthy cubs. That's at least half the number of wild snow leopards living in all of Russia!

Snow leopards born at the Bronx Zoo have been sent to zoos in seven countries and more than 30 U.S. states.

Buddhist Buddies

Buddhism is a world religion that honors love, respect, and compassion for all living beings. Buddhist monks are people who devote their whole lives to the religion. Many of these peaceful monks live high in the mountains of China, Nepal, and Mongolia, where most of the world's wild snow leopards live.

Buddhist monks have become the snow leopards' great protectors. They patrol the areas around their monasteries to keep people from hunting snow leopards. They use festivals and education programs to teach people how amazing and important snow leopards are. They even help researchers track the animals in their area. The monks believe snow leopards and their habitats are sacred, and they are helping to spread that message!

4

Tigers

Tigers are the biggest cats in the world!
Lions might be a little taller, but tigers
have more muscle. They are usually at
least sixty pounds heavier than lions.
The largest tigers can weigh almost 700
pounds. That's about the same as *ten* average ten-year-olds.

Tigers can
eat up to
75 pounds of
meat in one
sitting!

A tiger's body is long, too. From its
nose to its tailbone, a tiger is at least as
long as a motorcycle. Some are nearly the

length of a small car—and that doesn't include their tails! But you wouldn't want to get too close to a tiger with a ruler, because tigers have the longest fangs of any carnivore in the world.

Tiger fangs, or canine teeth, are about four inches long.

Habitat

There are fewer than 4,000 wild tigers left in the world. They are spread over thirteen different countries on the continent of Asia.

About half of the world's wild tigers are Bengal tigers.

Some, like Siberian tigers, can be found in the frozen forests of Russia. Others, like Bengal tigers, are found in the hot and steamy jungles of India. Some tigers live in grasslands. Others live in rocky regions. Tigers can survive almost anywhere if there is enough food and water nearby.

Unlike most cats, tigers seem to enjoy swimming! They have webbing between their toes to help them paddle through the water. Tigers can swim for miles and miles. Sometimes they swim to travel from one place to another. Sometimes they chase their prey into the water to catch it. But the main reason most tigers swim is to cool off.

Tigers usually swim with their heads above the water so they can keep track of what is happening around them.

Stripes and Spots

Tigers are probably best known for their orange fur and beautiful black-striped coats. Most tigers have at least a hundred stripes spread over their faces, sides, legs, and stomachs. The patterns of their

stripes are sort of like human fingerprints. No two are exactly alike. A tiger's skin is striped just like its fur. If you were to shave a tiger, it would still have its stripes. But, *please,* don't try to shave a tiger!

Stripes help tigers hide in tall grasses when they hunt. To their prey, the stripes look like harmless shadows. With this kind of camouflage, tigers can sneak up on their prey without being noticed.

If you think tigers' stripes are tricky, check out their eyespots! The eyespots, or *ocelli* (oh-SELL-eye), are round spots of white fur on the backs of each ear. They look just like wide-open eyes! Tigers are most in danger of being attacked when they are sleeping or bowing their heads to drink water. The eyespots trick other animals into thinking the tiger is awake and on the lookout.

This tiger's eyespots make it seem like it's staring straight ahead instead of drinking.

Cougar: The Cat of Many Names

Cougars can be found in at least sixteen states in the U.S., in western Canada, and in both Central and South America. People in these different regions often have their own names for this beautiful cat.

In many U.S. states, it's called a mountain lion, cougar, or catamount. In Florida, it's called a Florida panther. In Canada, it's usually known as a mountain lion. In Mexico and South America, it's often called a puma.

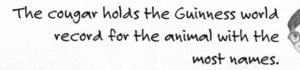

The cougar holds the Guinness world record for the animal with the most names.

A cougar is sometimes even called a mountain screamer because it makes calls that sound like a human scream! How did this cat get so many names? Mainly because it lives in so many places!

69

5

African Lions

The African lion is known as the king of the beasts. This fierce predator rules the savannas, or grassy plains, of Africa.

Lions have one of the animal kingdom's biggest bites—they can open their jaws up to eleven inches wide. They often attack animals much larger than themselves. Not even elephants are safe from lions!

Lion pride in Kenya

Prides

Lions are the only cats that live in groups. Their groups are called prides. Lion prides can have as few as three or as many as forty lions. On average, a pride includes two to three adult males, five to ten females, and their young. In a pride, lions work together to hunt, raise cubs, and defend their territory.

Female lions are called *lionesses*. They stay with the same pride their whole lives. Most females in a pride are related in some way—mothers, daughters, grandmothers, sisters, aunts, and cousins. They all share the cub-rearing duties.

Sometimes a single lioness will babysit all the cubs in the pride!

Lionesses also do most of the hunting. They work together as a team to take down large and fast animals like zebras, antelope, and buffalo. After a successful hunt, the entire pride gathers to share the meal. Adult male lions get first choice, then the adult females, and finally the cubs.

Male Lions
Male cubs stay with their pride until they are about two or three years old. Then they wander. They might survive on their own for a while, but they sometimes band together with other wandering males, often a couple of their brothers or half brothers. Once a young lion is fully mature, he will often take over a pride by forcing an older, weaker male to leave.

To gain control of a pride, younger male lions will fight older males, sometimes to the death.

While they are in their prime, male lions have two jobs. One is to father cubs, and the other is to guard the pride's territory from predators and other prides. No creature is strong enough to prey on adult male lions, but sometimes packs of wild dogs or hyenas will try to attack cubs. Males patrol the pride's land and kill or chase away any unwelcome visitors.

Male lions in the wild have a life span of about 8 to 10 years. In zoos, males can live up to 25 years!

Adult male lions rarely stay with a pride for more than a few years. They are either killed or kicked out by younger, stronger males looking to take over the pride. Older males that have been forced to leave their pride often join other banished males. These older bachelor groups often spend the rest of their lives wandering together.

Manes

Both male and female lions have short tawny-brown fur. It's easy to tell the difference between a lion and a lioness because males have manes. The shaggy fringe of hair around male lions' necks

makes them look much larger than females.

Manes are usually brownish and tinged with shades of rust and black. But the colors can change depending on the health of the lion. The strongest, healthiest lions have the darkest manes. These dark manes attract females and scare off male rivals. Illness, stress, or age can lighten mane color, which suggests a weaker lion.

Males also have tufts of black hair on the tips of their tails.

ROAR!

A lion's roar is as loud as a helicopter and can be heard up to five miles away! Lions roar for many reasons.

Different roars may all sound the same to us, but lions know how to tell them apart!

Speedy Cats

Cheetahs are the fastest land animals on earth. They can run as fast as seventy miles per hour! That's about three times as fast as the fastest human ever recorded! But cheetahs can only run at full speed for about thirty seconds. After that, they get too hot and must stop or slow down to catch their breath.

But even more amazing than the cheetah's top speed is its ability to *speed up quickly*. A cheetah can go from standing still to running at sixty miles per hour in just three seconds!

Only the fastest sports cars in the world can go from zero to sixty that quickly.

While running, cheetahs spend over half their time with all four paws off the ground.

6

Leopards and Jaguars

You can always tell a tiger by its stripes. Lions are easy to spot because they *don't* have spots or stripes, and males have shaggy manes. And snow leopards are the only big cats that are sometimes smoky-gray. But what about leopards and jaguars? Both are big cats. Both can roar. Both have sandy-colored fur with spots. So how can you tell which is which?

The easiest way to tell these cats apart is to know where you are! You'll never see leopards and jaguars together in the wild, because they live on different continents!

Leopards live mostly on the savannas of Africa. Some are found in many parts of Asia. But jaguars are found mostly in the rain forests of Central and South America.

There are occasional sightings of jaguars in the southwestern United States.

Bodies and Behavior

Geography isn't the only way to tell which spotted feline is which. If you listen carefully, you can hear the difference in their roars. A leopard's roar sounds like a saw going back and forth through a tree trunk. A jaguar's roar sounds like a deep, chesty cough.

You can also look closely at their bodies and behavior. The first thing you might notice is size.

Leopards are leaner than jaguars. They have longer legs and tails. Their long tails make them better at balancing in the treetops. Leopards often sleep draped over tree limbs. They also drag their prey into the trees to keep other animals from stealing their meal! Leopards mainly eat medium-size mammals, like antelope and deer. But they will also go after smaller prey, like birds, reptiles, and rodents.

Leopard

Jaguar

Jaguars are larger and heavier than leopards. Their bodies are barrel-shaped. They have a wider forehead. Their jaws are bigger and stronger. Jaguars can bite through the hides of crocodiles! Leopards can't. Jaguars eat up to eighty different kinds of animals, including snails, frogs, birds, deer, and monkeys. Also, jaguars like water and are very good swimmers.

Jaguars have one of the strongest bites of any mammal.

 Most cats sleep between 16 and 20 hours a day!

Fur

Since leopards and jaguars have similar fur color and patterns, does that mean it's impossible to tell their coats apart? Not if you look very closely at their markings.

 Leopard rosettes are small and tightly packed on most of the leopard's body.

On both cats, the rosettes are open black circles made up of lots of small spots. The fur color inside the spots is darker than the fur outside the spots.

Jaguar spots are a little larger and a little more spread out.

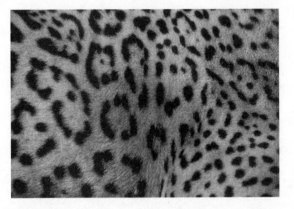

But a jaguar's rosettes are larger than a leopard's. And that isn't the only difference. Can you *spot* the best way to tell these cats apart? Yes! Jaguars have a black dot inside most of their rosettes!

Black Panthers

Did you know that there is no such thing as a black panther? But isn't that a black panther in the photo?

Actually, it's a jaguar! *Black panther* is just the term people use to refer to *any* big cat with a black coat. Most black panthers are really leopards or jaguars!

Pigments in a cat's fur and skin cause the light or dark markings. Sometimes these big cats are born with mostly dark pigments. When this happens, the spots of the leopard or jaguar disappear into the dark fur. But in the right light or up close, the spots can sometimes still be seen!

7

Small Wild Cats

Big cats are some of the most recognizable animals in the world. Even if you've never seen these famous felines in the wild or at the zoo, you've probably encountered them in books or movies. Small wild cats are not as well known or popular as their bigger cousins. But more than thirty species of cats are classified as small!

Some small wild cats are smaller than

Sand cats have such furry feet they don't leave paw prints when they walk! The fur protects their toe pads from burning on the hot sand.

house cats, like the five-pound sand cat. Some small cats are quite large, like the fifty-pound Eurasian lynx. None of the small cats can roar, but many have their own special skills.

The margay of the Amazon rain forest can mimic the call of a monkey. Margays use this vocal trick to lure monkeys closer to them so they can catch them and eat them. In South and Southeast Asia, fishing cats can scoop fish out of the water with their semi-webbed paws.

Whether they prowl deserts, rain forests, rocky mountains, or savanna grasslands, small wild cats are incredibly well adapted to their environment. They may be small, but they are no less amazing than big cats.

urn the page to meet :ome of our favorite small cats!

Rusty-Spotted Cat

The smallest feline in the world is the rusty-spotted cat. It is roughly half the size of an average house cat. An adult only weighs about two to three and a half pounds. When first born, a rusty-spotted kitten weighs less than a chicken's egg!

These tiny cats are found mostly in the forests of India and Sri Lanka. They are named for the rust-colored spots running down their backs. Their reddish-gray fur is short and soft. Their eyes are big and round.

Rusty-spotted cats may look like cute kitties, but they are fierce predators. They will attack prey up to three times their own size! They hunt rats, mice, lizards, and frogs. These cats are also great tree climbers. They can pounce on their prey from above and nab birds from the branches.

There are probably fewer than 10,000 rusty-spotted cats left in the wild, and only fifty-six live in zoos worldwide.

Caracal

Caracal comes from a Turkish word meaning "black ears." These medium-size cats weigh about thirty pounds, or as much as your average three-year-old. They are found throughout Africa and southwestern Asia. As their name suggests, caracals are best known for the tufts of black fur that spring from the tips of their long, pointy ears.

The long ear tufts direct sound waves into

the ears to boost hearing. Caracals also have over twenty different muscles to control the motion of each ear. The ears swivel to help pick up the faraway sounds of their prey.

Hearing is not their only hunting super-power. Caracals are incredibly high jump-ers. Their hind legs are long and strong and act like springs. In just one jump, they can leap ten feet to snatch birds out of the air.

Ocelot

Ocelots are about twice the size of an average house cat. They have one of the most beautiful coats of any animal in the world. Their sleek golden fur is covered with brown spots with black borders. They have dark stripes on their faces and black bands on their tails. It's easy to see why these cats are sometimes called painted leopards.

Ocelots are found in every country in South America except Chile. About fifty of these beautiful cats are left in the United States, mostly in Texas. Ocelots can thrive in wet, leafy rain forests as well as dry brush land.

Unlike many cats, they don't avoid water. Ocelots are good swimmers and can catch fish and frogs to eat.

Pallas's Cat

These furry, flat-faced felines are named after Peter Pallas. He was the German naturalist who first studied them.

Pallas's cats are native to central Asia. They live in many countries, including India, China, and Russia. They share habitats with snow leopards and have had to adapt to the same cold, dry, high-altitude environments.

Pallas's cats are about the size of an average house cat, but their thick fur makes them look much larger. They have the longest and thickest fur of all the small cats! Their fur helps keep them warm in freezing-cold weather.

Much like snow leopards, Pallas's cats are solitary creatures and are rarely seen in the wild. They spend most of their day in caves and rock crevices. They only come out at dusk to hunt. Researchers have given them the nickname *small ghosts of the mountain.*

These cats are best known for their grumpy facial expression. Their flat head; squinty brow; and tiny, wide-set ears make them look like they're always annoyed.

8

Wild Cats Today

Wild cats have lived on earth for millions of years. Sadly, nearly half of all the species of wild cats alive today are at risk of *extinction* (ick-STINK-shun). This means they could disappear from the world forever.

Most of the big cat populations are shrinking. There are only about 20,000 lions left in the wild. That number is half of what it was just twenty years ago. In the next twenty years, the number is likely to be cut in half again.

When the numbers become so small that a species is dangerously close to dying out, it is put on the *endangered species list*. When animals are put on the list, a government tries to protect them and their surroundings.

Some cats, like tigers, are on that list. Today there are fewer than 4,000 tigers left in the wild. Over the past hundred years, the world has lost about 95 percent of its tigers.

Snow leopards, lions, leopards, and cheetahs are on the *vulnerable* list. This means these cats are not in quite as much danger as tigers. But there is still a high risk of extinction.

Biggest Threats to Big Cats

Why does the number of big cats in the world keep getting smaller and smaller? Mostly because the number of humans in the world keeps getting bigger and bigger. There are over 7 billion people on the planet. That's more than ever before. Because the human population keeps growing, people are changing the land. They are destroying the habitats of many wild animals, including cats.

Two thousand trees are chopped down in the Amazon rain forest every minute.

Humans clear wild land for farming, mining, logging, factories, and homes. This forces the creatures that once lived on that land to leave. As their habitats shrink, big cats and other animals are forced into smaller and smaller areas. This makes it hard to find enough food and shelter to survive.

When big cats cannot find enough food in the wild, they may prey on livestock animals. Most herders are poor. So if a cat kills even just one of their animals, it is a terrible loss. This leads herders to kill big cats to protect their livestock.

Poachers often hunt animals to sell their body parts. The fur of snow leopards, tigers, and leopards can be sold for thousands of dollars. There are laws against big cats being killed so their fur can be sold, but some people break those laws. Buying poached animal parts is also illegal. If nobody bought fur and other parts, poachers would be out of business.

Hope

Humans are the greatest threat to big cats. But we can also be their greatest

One way people can work on saving snow leopards is to help herders build better fences to protect their livestock.

hope. One of the best ways to protect big cats is to teach people about how important they are. Big cats are beautiful and majestic creatures. And as top predators, they are necessary for the health of their habitats.

Think about snow leopards. If they died out, there would be too many wild goats and sheep on the mountains. This would lead to overgrazing of shrubs. The loss of shrubs would hurt the soil, leading to landslides and floods. If snow leopards are in danger, every living thing in and around their mountains is also in danger. Including humans.

This is what the monks know—and teach. Now you know it, too! So help spread the word about snow leopards and all the other amazing species of cats.

Doing More Research

There's a lot more you can learn about snow leopards and other wild cats. The fun of research is seeing how many different sources you can explore.

Books

Most libraries and bookstores have books about wild cats.

Here are some things to remember when you're using books for research:

1. You don't have to read the whole book. Check the table of contents and the index to find the topics you're interested in.

2. Write down the name of the book.
When you take notes, make sure you write down the name of the book in your notebook so you can find it again.

3. Never copy exactly from a book.
When you learn something new from a book, put it in your own words.

4. Make sure the book is <u>nonfiction</u>.
Some books tell make-believe stories about wild cats. Make-believe stories are called *fiction*. They're fun to read, but not good for research.

Research books have facts and tell true stories. They are called *nonfiction*. A librarian or teacher can help you make sure the books you use for research are nonfiction.

Here are some good nonfiction books about snow leopards and other wild cats:

- *The Big Book of Wild Cats* (Fun Animal Facts for Kids) by Rachael Smith
- *Big Cats* by Seymour Simon
- *Everything Big Cats* by Elizabeth Carney
- *Face to Face with Lions* by Beverly and Dereck Joubert
- *Snow Leopards* (Amazing Animals) by Valerie Bodden
- *Wild Cats* (Step into Reading) by Mary Batten

Zoos and Museums

Many zoos and museums can help you learn more about snow leopards and other wild cats.

When you go to a museum:

1. Be sure to take your notebook!
Write down anything that catches your interest. Draw pictures, too!

2. Ask questions.
There are almost always people at zoos and museums who can help you find what you're looking for.

3. Check the calendar.
Many zoos and museums have special events and activities just for kids!

115

Here are some zoos and museums where you can learn about wild cats:

- American Museum of Natural History (New York)
- Bronx Zoo (New York)
- Cincinnati Zoo
- Harvard Museums of Science & Culture (Cambridge, MA)
- San Diego Zoo

The Internet

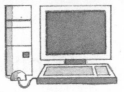

Many websites have lots of facts about snow leopards and other wild cats. Some also have activities that can help make learning about wild cats easier.

Ask your teacher or your parents to help you find more websites like these:

- kids.nationalgeographic.com/animals /mammals/facts/snow-leopard
- nationalgeographic.org/projects/big-cats -initiative/how-you-can-help
- online.kidsdiscover.com/unit/big-cats
- panthera.org
- snowleopard.org

Bibliography

Brown, Sarah. *The Cat: A Natural and Cultural History.* New Jersey: Princeton University Press, 2020.

Castelló, José R. *Felids and Hyenas of the World: Wild Cats, Panthers, Lynx, Pumas, Ocelots, Caracals, and Relatives.* New Jersey: Princeton University Press, 2020.

Hallet, Mark, and John M. Harris. *On the Prowl: In Search of Big Cat Origins.* New York: Columbia University Press, 2020.

Hunter, Luke. *Wild Cats of the World.* London: Bloomsbury Wildlife, 2015.

Kidd, Shavaun Mara, with Björn Persson, eds. *Searching for the Snow Leopard: Guardian of the High Mountains.* New York: Arcade Publishing, 2020.

Sunquist, Fiona, and Mel Sunquist. *The Wild Cat Book: Everything You Ever Wanted to Know About Cats.* Chicago: The University of Chicago Press, 2014.

Index

Photographs courtesy of:

*Have you read the adventure that
matches up with this book?*

Don't miss
Magic Tree House® #36
Sunlight on the Snow Leopard

The magic tree house takes Jack and Annie to
Nepal with a mission to find . . . a ghost! But
what does this have to do with a mountain, an
old man, and a snow leopard?

Magic Tree House®

#1: Dinosaurs Before Dark
#2: The Knight at Dawn
#3: Mummies in the Morning
#4: Pirates Past Noon
#5: Night of the Ninjas
#6: Afternoon on the Amazon
#7: Sunset of the Sabertooth
#8: Midnight on the Moon
#9: Dolphins at Daybreak
#10: Ghost Town at Sundown
#11: Lions at Lunchtime
#12: Polar Bears Past Bedtime
#13: Vacation Under the Volcano
#14: Day of the Dragon King
#15: Viking Ships at Sunrise
#16: Hour of the Olympics
#17: Tonight on the *Titanic*
#18: Buffalo Before Breakfast
#19: Tigers at Twilight
#20: Dingoes at Dinnertime
#21: Civil War on Sunday
#22: Revolutionary War on Wednesday
#23: Twister on Tuesday
#24: Earthquake in the Early Morning
#25: Stage Fright on a Summer Night
#26: Good Morning, Gorillas
#27: Thanksgiving on Thursday
#28: High Tide in Hawaii
#29: A Big Day for Baseball
#30: Hurricane Heroes in Texas
#31: Warriors in Winter
#32: To the Future, Ben Franklin!
#33: Narwhal on a Sunny Night
#34: Late Lunch with Llamas
#35: Camp Time in California
#36: Sunlight on the Snow Leopard

Magic Tree House® Merlin Missions

#1: Christmas in Camelot
#2: Haunted Castle on Hallows Eve
#3: Summer of the Sea Serpent
#4: Winter of the Ice Wizard
#5: Carnival at Candlelight
#6: Season of the Sandstorms
#7: Night of the New Magicians
#8: Blizzard of the Blue Moon
#9: Dragon of the Red Dawn
#10: Monday with a Mad Genius
#11: Dark Day in the Deep Sea
#12: Eve of the Emperor Penguin
#13: Moonlight on the Magic Flute
#14: A Good Night for Ghosts
#15: Leprechaun in Late Winter
#16: A Ghost Tale for Christmas Time
#17: A Crazy Day with Cobras
#18: Dogs in the Dead of Night
#19: Abe Lincoln at Last!
#20: A Perfect Time for Pandas
#21: Stallion by Starlight
#22: Hurry Up, Houdini!
#23: High Time for Heroes
#24: Soccer on Sunday
#25: Shadow of the Shark
#26: Balto of the Blue Dawn
#27: Night of the Ninth Dragon

Magic Tree House®
Super Edition

#1: WORLD AT WAR, 1944

Magic Tree House®
Fact Trackers

More Magic Tree House®

Explore the world with

MAGIC TREE HOUSE

HOME ADVENTURES!

Join Jack and Annie on exciting adventures all from the comfort of your home!

DISCOVER CRAFTS, RECIPES, GAMES, VIDEOS, AND MORE!

Explore more at
GOMAGICTREEHOUSE.COM today!